What Do Dogs Know?

What Do Dogs Know?

STANLEY COREN AND JANET WALKER

ILLUSTRATED BY PIERRE LE TAN

Illustrations Inspired by Janet Walker

SIMON & SCHUSTER
A VIACOM COMPANY

First published in the USA by The Free Press, 1997
A division of Simon & Schuster Inc.

First published in Great Britain by Simon & Schuster UK Ltd, 1998
A Viacom company

1 3 5 7 9 10 8 6 4 2

Simon & Schuster Ltd
West Garden Place
Kendal Street
London W2 2AQ

Simon & Schuster Australia
Sydney

A CIP catalogue record for this book is available from the British Library

ISBN 0-684-84860-0

Printed in Hong Kong by Midas Printing Ltd.

With love for Jessie, Kona, Odin and Wiz,

the dogs who know us today;

and in memory of

Flint and Chris,

who knew us just a short time ago.

Contents

Introduction

What do we know about dogs? As a behavioral scientist and dog trainer who has spent many years studying dogs, I can say that we know quite a bit about their behavior, history and mental processes. Unfortunately, though, what we think we know is not always as clear as we would like it to be.

For instance, where do dogs come from? Various scientists claim, each with a reasonable degree of certainty, that dogs may or may not have begun as domesticated wolves. Dogs may or may not be derived from jackals. It is also true that dogs may or may not be descendants of coyotes, dingos or African wild dogs. Of course any combination of these is also possible, since each of these "wild" species can successfully cross-breed with dogs to produce perfectly sound (although often bizarre-looking) puppies.

We do know that for at least fourteen thousand years, dogs have been partners with humans. This alliance began with Neanderthal man—not exactly stimulating company, perhaps, but presumably early dogs found him to be a better companion than anything else on earth at the time. When evolution brought about Cro-Magnon man, dogs must have immediately sensed the potential in the new, improved human model.

Some authorities have speculated that when Neanderthals were abandoned by dogs and left to shift for themselves, they became desperate and tried to domesticate cats. (This unfortunate decision may explain why, shortly thereafter, Neanderthals disappeared completely.)

Cro-Magnon man and dogs made an excellent team, and before long they were grilling antelope steaks over something called fire. Sometime later, the humans moved into caves and learned to trap the fire in hearths. Once dogs had comfortably settled themselves in front of the hearth, the dog and human coalition was permanently established. Thousands of years later, when "civilized" men crossed the Atlantic Ocean and arrived on the shores of North America, they brought with them alcohol, syphilis, trousers, the Bible, and dogs. All were new to the natives—except dogs.

We know quite a bit about the way dogs' minds work, although far from enough to conclude that we actually understand these animals. For instance, we know that dogs are more intelligent than horses, cats, dolphins and some politicians. The best guess is that the average dog is almost as smart as a two-year-old child—and maybe a bit better in toilet-training skills.

We know that dogs feel emotions. They definitely feel joy, fear and anger; experts argue about whether dogs feel grief and remorse as well. Dogs also may or may not feel jealousy, ambition, humbleness, smugness or a desire to star in slapstick home videos.

We know that dogs understand language—but how much? One researcher claims that his dogs could only learn 22 words. Another scientist claims that dogs can understand 65 words, and further research suggests that there may be 110, 140, 165 or up to 300 words in a dog's vocabulary. Meanwhile, I have seen a dog on television that sings "O Sole Mio" with better pronunciation of the Italian language than I can manage.

We are still learning about the complex interaction between dogs and humans. We know that the canine pact with man involves dogs giving up their freedom, but not their independence. We also know that dogs are more loyal to their human friends than to their own convictions, and perhaps more loyal to us than we deserve.

Given this mixed state of knowledge, we will devote ourselves in this book to exploring the question: "What do dogs know?" We will also ask some other important questions: What do dogs think about themselves? What do they think of those large two-legged creatures they share their lives with? Do dogs have a philosophy of life? In the pages that follow we will give you a set of facts, stories and simple musings that may—or may not—answer some of these questions.

CHAPTER 1

How Do Dogs Think?

I have often watched my dogs while they play, rest or merely observe the world. As a psychologist I have seen evidence that dogs can think and reason and feel emotions, but what do they really *know?* What goes through a dog's mind as it looks out a window?

Near me now are four dogs; my two, and the two that belong to my wife's daughter, Karen. Like most people, I believe I can tell what my family's dogs are thinking about or feeling, just by looking at them. To me it is obvious that Tessa, lying on the porch, is watching for intruders—ready to sound the alarm, as always. My flat-coat retriever, Odin, is scanning the trees, watching hopefully for birds. The youngest, Bishop, is slowly sneaking up on our cat, Loki, with either play or malice in his mind. But then there is my inscrutable old dog, Wiz. His tail gently thumps on the floor as he sits and stares intently at a blank wall. This is common behavior for him. Is he, like some Eastern philosophers, contemplating the mysterious purity of nothingness? Is he in some state of Zen meditation? Has he merely paused in this place to formulate his plans for the day? My wife passes by, looks at him, and comments, "You know, your dog looks like his brain has closed down again." Wiz keeps thumping his tail. He may not be thinking—but he's happy.

$\mathscr{S}$ome scientists are convinced that dogs cannot really think or reason; all of the behaviors that your dog engages in are therefore supposed to be done without thought, planning or insight. These experts still believe the theories of the French philosopher Descartes, who described dogs as machines, filled with the biological equivalent of gears and pulleys. Like other machines they don't think, but they can be programmed to do certain things.

Some say that Descartes had a hidden agenda. For if dogs can think, and if they have consciousness—then, according to church doctrine, they must also have souls. Anything with a soul is eligible for entry into Heaven, of course, and some members of the clergy were becoming concerned about possible overcrowding in Paradise. Machines, however, have no souls; therefore one need not allow an Akita-shaped automaton or a mechanized Maltese to pass through the Pearly Gates of Heaven. As a by-product, one assumes, there would be no necessity to institute leash laws for dogs exercising on the Elysian Fields.

*S*ome other experts feel that dogs are capable of reasoning and have the same kinds of mental processes that people do—although, perhaps, somewhat simpler in nature. For them, dogs are almost equivalent to four-footed humans in fur coats. A number of cultures (including the Ainu of Japan, the Kalang of Java, and the Niasese of Sumatra) have stories claiming that dogs are really the ancestors of humans.

In some Tibetan monasteries, a dog is brought into the room of a dying priest. The monks believe that the dog will serve as a temporary home for the soul of the holy man until he can be reincarnated in a new human body. Some religious sects go ever further, believing that all dogs are people who will be restored to human form in the afterlife. Scientists, however, are in reasonable agreement that under a dog's fur coat we will find only a dog.

Researchers have proven that the nerve cells in a dog's brain work the same as those in a human brain. The neurons that make up the human brain have the same chemical composition as the neurons in a dog and the patterns of electrical activity are identical. The dog's brain also contains most of the same structures that are found in the brain of a person.

Like humans, dogs have special areas of the brain that are set aside for specific activities. In fact, if we drew a map of the locations of various functions in the dog's brain, it would be remarkably similar to the map for those same functions in the human brain. For instance, vision is located at the very back of the brain in both species. Humans and dogs both locate the areas responsible for hearing at the side of the brain, near the temples. The sense of touch and control of movements are located in a thin strip running over the top of the brain.

If we look beyond the microscopic level, however, there are some important differences between the brain of a dog and the brain of a person. Indeed, psychologists believe that as much as 60 percent of the human brain is set aside for processing conscious thoughts, interpreting and producing language or storing memories and solving problems. Many dog owners believe that as much as 60 percent of their pet's brain is set aside solely to demonstrate applications of the verb "to eat"—in both the active and the passive forms.

*M*any ancient sages had a very high opinion of the dog's intellect. The Greek philosopher Plato described the "noble dog" as "a lover of learning" and "a beast worthy of wonder."

His contemporary Diogenes was a bit of an eccentric; he was known for wandering the world with a lamp while looking for a honest man. Believing that dogs were extremely intelligent, Diogenes even adopted the nickname "Cyon" (which means "dog"). As a result, when he founded one of the great ancient schools of philosophy, Diogenes and his followers were known by his nickname as "Cynics" (or "dog thinkers"). When he died, the Athenians raised a great marble pillar in his memory, with the image of a dog at the top. Underneath, a long inscription started with the following bit of conversation:

"Say, Dog, I pray, what guard you in that tomb?"

"A dog."

"His name?"

"Diogenes."

While the question of how intelligent dogs are remains a matter of great scientific debate, we do know that sometimes dogs can do things that humans could never teach them. Take the rescue dogs that were named for the hospice at the Saint Bernard pass in the Swiss Alps.

The Saint Bernards work best in teams of at least three dogs. They are sent out on patrols following storms, and they wander the paths looking for stranded travelers. If they come upon a victim, two dogs lie down beside the person to keep him warm; one of the two licks his face to stimulate him back to consciousness. Meanwhile, another dog will have already started back to the hospice to sound the alarm and guide the monks to the scene.

These dogs are never given any special training—in fact, no one is sure exactly how you would train a dog to do all this. Young dogs learn what is expected of them simply by running with the older dogs on patrol. Ultimately, each dog decides for itself whether its job will be to lie with the victim or go for help. Incidentally, the classic image of a Saint Bernard dog with a keg of brandy attached to its collar is a myth. It was the hospice monks who carried the brandy to help warm the chilled travelers.

*S*ometimes people give dogs credit for knowing more than they actually do. Take the case of Kato, the Akita owned by Nicole Brown Simpson. As probably everyone one this planet knows, the murder of Nicole and her friend Ron Goldman triggered one of the most publicized and controversial trials in history because the accused killer was the sports hero and actor O.J. Simpson.

Kato enters the story because one of the neighbors heard the dog's agitated whining on the night of the murders. Noticing blood on Kato's paws, the man assumed the dog had injured itself. As the neighbor tried to return Kato to Nicole's home, the dog pulled him in the direction of the garage; this was how the bodies were discovered. Many people felt that Kato had seen the murder and was trying to get help.

One morning, while O.J. Simpson's trial was in progress, I received a phone call from a lawyer associated with the court proceedings. He offered me a lot of money if I would come to Los Angeles, meet with Kato, and see if I could get the dog to identify the murderer. I tried to explain that in comparison to humans, dogs have a mental ability similar to that of a two-year-old child. I asked him if he would expect a human two-year-old—with no clear understanding of death, and limited language ability— to be able to comment on an event that occurred nine months earlier. "Look," he pleaded, "couldn't you just come down and interview the dog?" Forgetting that some lawyers lack a sense of humor, I quipped, "You mean something like getting him to bark once for yes and twice for no?" The amazed voice on the phone asked, "Could you do that?"

had a similar experience when I served as the master of ceremonies for a series of dog demonstrations held at the Pacific Canine Exhibition. The acts included a dog that herded ducks, one that did scent discrimination, others that performed agility tricks, some that jumped, and even a pair of dogs that danced with their masters.

For comic relief we had Rupert, a lovable, lop-eared basset hound. In rehearsals, I quickly taught Rupert that food treats might be found in several places around the stage. At various times he would be released during an act—wandering around leisurely and (as far as anyone else could tell) aimlessly, but really searching for the food. This would serve as the opportunity for some funny banter.

During the actual show, while a Labrador retriever was demonstrating his ability to catch three tennis balls in his mouth at once, Rupert sauntered across the stage once more. Having ingested quite a few treats by then, he stopped in the middle of the floor and relieved himself. The crowd roared with embarrassed laughter. Making the best of the situation, I mock-scolded him over the microphone: "Now Rupert! Stop that and act like a gentleman!" Apparently Rupert's bottom itched from the previous activity, because he put his rear end down on the floor and dragged himself across the stage and out of sight, using only his front legs. The crowd laughed wildly, and again I improvised, saying, "Rupert, have you forgotten how to act politely?"—at which moment he reappeared, still dragging his bottom, moving in the return direction across the stage. The auditorium collapsed in noisy giggles.

After the show I was approached by two well-known Canadian dog trainers, who told me they were quite impressed. What they really wanted to know, though, was how I had trained Rupert to do "all that."

cientists have shown that dogs think in concrete rather than abstract terms. One psychologist tried to see if dogs have any knowledge of numbers. He made a set of little balls of hamburger meat and put them in groups in different locations on the floor. The number of meat balls in the groups differed, so that one might have a single ball of meat, while another might have three or four balls. The psychologist reasoned that if dogs could count and understood fundamental notions associated with quantities (for example, that four is greater than one) then given the choice of different piles, a dog would select the one with the largest number of meatballs.

What this researcher found was that when the groups of meatballs were at different distances, the dog being tested was very practical—he simply grabbed the closest pile, regardless of its size. Only if there were two groups of meatballs at the same distance did dogs consider the number, and then they did grab the one with the highest count. However, even if dogs have the basic concept of size or number, it is probably a waste of time to ask your dog about higher mathematics. He probably thinks that geometry is some kind of new biscuit, and algebra is a three-cornered dog toy.

n older books that mention dogs, the writers refer to them as "dumb brutes." It is important to remember that they used the word "dumb" to indicate an inability to speak and use language, not a lack of intelligence. Dogs seem to know that people often like to be in the company of someone who is not as bright or educated as themselves. Such encounters evoke, in the brighter individual, a feeling of love and protectiveness for the dull-witted one. For this reason, I would suggest that dogs often cultivate a sort of stupid, "I-don't-have-a-clue-what-is-going-on-around-here" look. Dogs feel that this makes us humans feel more superior and more relaxed around them.

Actually, being ignorant with an equally ignorant friend can sometimes be quite comforting as well. For instance, I know that most of the philosophical discussions that I have with my dog are not very impressive, since neither I nor my canine companion know what I am talking about. This fact, however, does not stop me from enjoying the serenity and companionship that such conversations with my friend bring.

*J*ust as the brain structure of humans has much in common with that of dogs, our mental processes also have many similarities. For example, one mental process that dogs share with us is that they dream much the way that we do. Of course, dogs dream only doggy things. We know this because there is a special structure in the brain that keeps all of us from acting out our dreams. In experiments when scientists have removed that part of the brain from dogs, the animals would start to move around when they were dreaming. This occurred despite the fact that electrical recordings of their brains indicated that they were still fast asleep. As these dogs moved, they actually began to act out the actions they were performing in their dreams. Thus researchers found that a dreaming pointer might immediately start searching for game (and might even go on point), a sleeping springer spaniel might flush an imaginary bird, while the slumbering Doberman pinscher might pick a fight with a dream burglar.

You can tell when your dog is dreaming by watching him. When he first falls asleep, his breathing will become more regular as the sleep becomes deeper. When the dream starts, the dog's breathing becomes shallow and irregular. There may be occasional muscle twitches, and you can actually see his eyes moving behind his closed lids if you look closely enough. The eyes are moving because the dog is actually looking at the dream images in the same way that he would look at real objects in the outside world.

Not all dogs dream equally. It is an odd fact that small dogs dream more frequently than big dogs. A dog as small as a toy poodle may dream once every ten minutes, while a dog as large as a mastiff or an Irish wolfhound may spend an hour and a half between each dream. Just as with humans, the amount of time dogs spend dreaming depends on their age. Young puppies spend more of their sleep time dreaming than do adult dogs.

The amount of sleep that an animal needs depends upon its species. Horses and cows may sleep only three or four hours daily, while bats and opossums may sleep closer to 20 hours. The various breeds of dogs also seem to have different sleep requirements.

Some very large breeds of dogs, like Newfoundlands, Saint Bernards, and mastiffs, often spend a great deal of their lives sleeping—perhaps up to sixteen or even eighteen hours a day. For this reason they were often referred to as "mat dogs," because they could always be found lying in front of the fireplace (much like a giant, furry hearth mat). If it is true that dogs dream about what they do, then we must conclude that Great Danes probably only dream about sleeping.

Some old folk traditions say that human dreams sometimes can be used to foretell the future. For people who believe in such forecasts, dreams about dogs have special meanings. As in the case of most prophesies the trick is to figure out the message conveyed by the dogs in your dreams. Dreams of dogs barking are supposed to be good omens, while dreams of dogs howling are supposed to be bad omens. Calpurnia, the wife of Julius Caesar had a dream that included a yellow dog howling and because of this she tried to keep Caesar home that day. He ignored her fears and set out that morning on the fateful walk to the Senate where he would meet Brutus and his co-conspirators.

Small differences in the nature of the dream dog can have special significance, such as its color. Thus a black or gray dog in a dream is said to mean misfortune while a red dog with white markings can mean speedy recovery from illness. A dream of a white dog can mean victory. In 1942, General George S. Patton was leading the U.S. 1st Armor Corps in its invasion of North Africa. One morning he awakened and told his aide, "Last night I had a dream about a big white dog. I don't know what it means, but I know that I am that dog." Later that afternoon he went on to have his first major victory in a pitched tank battle against German General Erwin Rommel's Afrika Corps.

CHAPTER 2

What Do Dogs Sense?

*D*ogs and humans obviously differ in many ways. One of the most important differences is in how the two species perceive the world. For instance, dogs have an incredible ability to read scents. If you could unfold the inner surface of a dog's nose (the part with the cells that allow the dog to smell), it would actually cover a surface area larger than the entire extent of the dog's skin.

Dogs read the state of the world through their noses, and they write their messages to other dogs in urine. A particular dog's urine contains a lot of information about that dog. It smells different depending upon the dog's age and health; whether it is male or female, or a female in heat; and even depending upon the dog's emotional state. For a dog, sniffing a fire hydrant or a tree along a route popular with other dogs is a means of keeping abreast of current events. That tree is really a large newspaper containing the latest news items in the dog world, and perhaps even installments of classic canine literature.

*A*ny discussion of dogs' sense of smell ultimately leads to the greatest, most imponderable question about dogs—the question that nags at children and leaves their parents groping for an appropriate answer: why do they have wet noses?

Scientists have many answers for this. One is that the evaporation of moisture from the nose helps cool the dog. Another is that added moisture in the nose makes the dog more sensitive to odors. The most boring answer is that many dogs simply lick their noses with their tongues, thus wetting them.

A folk tale that goes back to biblical times gives yet another answer. When God flooded the world, the story goes, all life on the planet was inside of Noah's ark. The two dogs Noah had chosen constantly patrolled the ark, checking on the other animals, and generally just poking around as dogs do. One day, the dogs were taking their daily stroll when they noticed a coin-sized leak, through which water was rushing in at a rapid rate. One dog quickly ran for help, while the other dog gallantly stuck his nose in the hole to plug it. By the time Noah and his sons arrived to repair the hole, the poor dog was in great pain and gasping for breath, but a major disaster had been averted. According to this tale, dogs' cold, wet noses are simply a badge of honor, conferred upon them by God in memory of that heroic act.

For dogs, beauty is taken in by the nose in the same way that for humans it comes through the eyes. People often wonder why an otherwise apparently sane dog would roll around in garbage or dung. Scientists say that this behavior might be an attempt at disguise passed down by the dog's wild ancestors, who had to hunt for a living. If an antelope smelled the scent of a wild dog nearby, it would be likely to bolt and run for safety. For this reason the dogs would roll in antelope dung. Antelopes are quite used to the odor of their own droppings and therefore are not suspicious of a hairy thing coated with that smell. This allows the wild hunting canine to get much closer to its prey. Personally, I suspect that the real reason dogs roll in obnoxious-smelling organic matter today is probably an expression of the same sense of aesthetics that causes human beings to wear loud Hawaiian shirts.

*C*ompared to their sense of smell, dogs seem to pay a lot less attention to their sense of taste. Apparently they believe that if something fits into their mouths, then it is food, no matter what it tastes like. In this, however, they are wrong. Several common forms of people food are bad for dogs. Probably one of the worst offenders is chocolate, in part because people think that they are being nice to their dogs by giving them a bit of chocolate as a treat. (In addition, chocolates are everywhere during holiday seasons, and it is easy to leave an open box of chocolates on a low table within easy reach of a dog's mouth.) The caffeine and theobromine (a related compound) contained in a single milk chocolate bar can make a ten-pound dog very sick. Because darker chocolate means a higher concentration of these compounds, an equal amount of baker's chocolate can kill that same ten-pound dog. Onion and garlic are also on the banned list of dog foods. The large amount of sulfur in these vegetables can destroy red blood cells in dogs, causing severe anemic reactions.

Even things that are not food can be tempting to dogs. In Australia, an eighteen-month-old boxer named Kizzy had been eating poorly, and the medications prescribed by her veterinarian didn't help. Kizzy's owners brought her to another veterinarian, who decided to operate. He retrieved a twelve-inch bread knife from the dog's belly! Amazingly, there was no serious damage, and at last report Kizzy was recovering well.

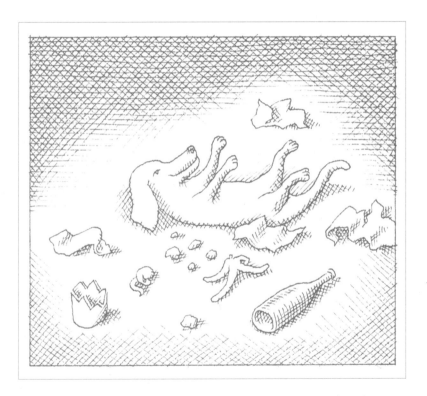

*M*ost people know that a dog's hearing is much more sensitive than that of humans, but they may not know that the nature of the sounds dogs hear is also much different. Dogs can hear much higher tones; even the most sensitive people can't hear above 20,000 cycles per second, while some dogs can hear above 45,000. The "silent whistles" sometimes used to signal dogs are not really silent, but their sound is at around 25,000 cycles per second—too high for humans to hear, but not for dogs.

Smaller dogs can actually hear higher tones than bigger dogs. It has to do with the size of their ears. Small ears are more sensitive to high-pitched tones because a resonance in the ear amplifies these high sounds. On the other hand, dogs with big, square, mastiff-type heads (including Saint Bernards) can hear sub-sonic tones. These are very low frequency sounds—far too low for humans to hear. Thus Saint Bernards are able to hear the faint low frequency sounds made by people trapped under snow by avalanches, which dogs with smaller heads cannot sense at all. Some can even hear the very low sounds made when a body of snow starts to move over ice or rock. This is why some Saint Bernards have been successful at giving warnings of an impending avalanche several minutes before it is detectable by people.

One television program I saw attempted to show that dogs were musical. It showed video clips of dogs howling while their masters played a violin, clarinet or piano. This reminded me of a film clip I had once seen with President Lyndon Baines Johnson sitting in the Oval Office of the White House with a mixed-breed terrier named Yuki on his lap. Johnson was lustily singing a Western folk song but he was hideously off-key. Yuki was accompanying him with yips and howls that were at least as musical as the cacophony made by the President.

Another president, Franklin Delano Roosevelt, claimed that he witnessed a performance of one of the world's greatest musical dogs. In 1936, FDR invited the Golden Gloves boxing champion Arthur "Stubby" Stubbs and his pit bull terrier, Bud, to the White House. He later reported that while Stubby played the banjo, Bud sang a medley of Stephen Foster songs.

The truth is that dogs may not really like music at all, but they absolutely love the noise it makes. If dogs were patrons of the arts, they would hire composers to write music like Wagner—only louder.

This is not to say that dogs have no sense of tone or song. There is a certain musicality within all canines, from domestic dogs to their wild relatives. This shows up in their howls.

One reason why dogs and wolves howl may be loneliness. They are basically asking, "Is there anybody out there?" They also answer another dog's howl with a "yip howl," where the long, mournful howling note is preceded by two or three yipping sounds. This yip howl says "I'm here." The original howler will then change his own song to a yip howl in response.

Once the yip howling begins, it often turns into a joyous celebration. The dogs or wolves are happily announcing their own presence and their camaraderie with others of their species in what might be termed a spontaneous canine jam session. This vocal performance may go on for quite a while and involve animals from all over a region or a neighborhood.

It is during such a wild concert that canines show their musical sensitivity. Recordings of wolves have shown that a howling wolf will change its tone when others join the chorus. No wolf seems to want to end up on the same note as any other in the choir.

When it comes to vision, humans are considerably better off than their canine companions. Dogs can never know much about colors, since their color vision is limited; indeed, for many years scientists thought that dogs could only see the world in shades of gray.

Recent research has proven that dogs do have some color vision. This was done by training dogs to discriminate between various colored lights. These studies determined that our pet canines can't tell the difference between reds and greens at all, and they probably see the world in shades of blue and yellow.

The effort it took to train dogs in these experimental tests probably means that dogs don't attach the significance to colors that humans do. For instance, take an old brown sofa that a dog likes to curl up in and reupholster it in a delicate, light blue fabric. Suddenly the dog's family won't let him come near it anymore. Dogs are unclear about the concept here. They may wonder, "Is light blue dangerous or unhealthy for dogs?"

find it almost impossible to talk about the color vision of dogs without mentioning the case of Bill Bowen and his guide dog, Bud. Bowen had been declared legally blind, since all he had was the scant remainder of some peripheral vision. That's why he needed Bud to guide him through his daily activities.

In 1984, Bowen was arrested for drunken driving; he was found in the front seat of a car that had been weaving erratically all over the road. When he was brought before a judge, Bowen testified that he was only the passenger—Bud had actually been driving. The judge, who clearly knew a bit about dogs, was skeptical: "The witnesses say that the car did stop when the traffic lights turned red, and started again when they turned green. How could Bud do that, since dogs are color blind?" Bowen was unfazed by this question. "Bud has learned the positions of the lights," he said. "He knows that he is supposed to stop when the top light is lit and go if the bottom one is on."

The court case was just about to move to the next stage when Bowen broke down and admitted that he had lied. He said that he had in fact been both drinking and driving, and now he was ashamed for trying to frame his loyal guide dog. "I still don't understand," said the judge. "If you are blind, then how did you read the traffic lights?" "Well," said Bowen, "That really was Bud. He was in the passenger seat, and he just barked once to tell me the light was green and twice to tell me the light was red."

*G*enerally speaking, dogs are not as visually oriented as people. They certainly do not have the fascination that people do with mirrors. Most young puppies will respond to their own image in a mirror the first time they see it. Usually, however, they lose interest in it after only a few minutes. From that time on, dogs will completely ignore their own reflection.

On the other hand, some dogs seem to like to watch television. Evidence shows that dogs much prefer European television, where the image is much sharper due to a higher scanning frequency (625 lines per second, as opposed to 525 lines in the American television system). Dogs' visual acuity is good enough to perceive the American signal as wavy, less stable, and therefore less realistic.

Nonetheless, there are special videos made for entertaining dogs. One of the most popular of these is shot from a dog's-eye-level view, and it includes such activities as watching a tennis game, chasing a cat, and looking at some birds. When it comes to broadcast television programs, one survey found that for dogs, the top-ranking TV shows included Oprah Winfrey, David Letterman and "Wheel of Fortune." Dogs' favorite TV movies seem to be anything by the Marx Brothers, the Three Stooges or Bugs Bunny. A dog day-care center in New York (which operates under the name of "Yuppy Puppy") keeps its charges happy by continuously playing Marx Brothers films on floor-level TV screens.

*D*ogs seem to have other senses that humans do not possess. Researchers think dogs may be able to sense the coming of earthquakes, even before sensitive scientific equipment can. For instance, there was a sudden increase in the number of dogs reported to have run away from home in the few days before the most recent earthquakes in San Francisco and Los Angeles.

One dog expert suggested that this sudden exodus of family pets occurred because the dogs were sensing something that they wanted to escape—presumably the impending cataclysm. Some scientists think that dogs might have a means of detecting changes in the magnetic fields around them, while others believe that their ears may be sensitive enough to actually hear the faint cracking and snapping sounds coming from the region of the earth where the pressure builds up before the quake. In a similar vein, there are reports of dogs becoming upset and agitated enough to seek shelter from approaching tornados or hurricanes, long before their masters become aware of the danger.

*D*ogs can certainly sense other things that humans can't. Take the case of Harley, a golden retriever owned by Victoria Doroshenko.

Harley seems to have incredible medical sensitivity. Victoria is an epileptic, and Harley warns her of oncoming seizures long before she—or anyone else—can see symptoms. How he recognizes them is not clear; Perhaps he senses small behavioral changes, tiny shifts in her body condition, or possibly changes in odor, sweating or other secretions, or maybe even changes in her brain waves. No matter how he does it, he is a medical miracle. Victoria says, "Before I got my dog, I was afraid and housebound. Harley gave me my life back." Harley is not alone in his abilities. There is now even a Seizure Alert Dog Association that trains other dogs to perform the same service that Harley does.

*D*ogs can sense more than just oncoming seizures. Richard Simmons, a research associate working on a project supported in part by the U.S. National Institutes of Health, told me a story about Marilyn Zuckerman of New York and her Shetland sheepdog, Tricia.

Tricia had developed the annoying habit of sniffing or nuzzling Marilyn's lower back whenever she sat down. Marilyn's husband looked and noticed that there was a dark mole in the location that Tricia seemed to be interested in. It seemed odd that the dog cared about this mole, but since it caused no discomfort, Marilyn just ignored it. One spring day, though, Marilyn was lying face down on her balcony in a bathing suit, simply enjoying the sunshine—when suddenly she felt teeth on her back. It was Tricia, who apparently was trying to remove the mole.

Marilyn's husband suggested that there must be something odd about the mole if it was bothering the dog that much. More out of curiosity than anything else, Marilyn showed it to her doctor. Before the day was out, Marilyn was at the Cornell Medical Center, where the mole was diagnosed as skin cancer—actually a virulent and potentially fatal form of melanoma. Tricia's early warning probably saved Marilyn's life.

As Simmons told me: "It was because of stories like Marilyn's that we began testing dogs' diagnostic abilities. Our preliminary data suggests that dogs can detect melanomas and several other types of cancer well before there is any other indication of a problem. Some dogs will show agitation the moment a person with cancer enters the room. It may well be that someday in the future, inspection by a dog may become a routine part of cancer screening."

$\mathcal{S}$ome people even think that dogs have ESP and the ability to sense the spirit world. One British scientist suggested that dogs use this ability to sense when their owners are coming home. To demonstrate this, he installed hidden video cameras in the homes of dog owners.

Most of the time, these cameras simply recorded the dog sleeping. However, the dogs would get up and start to hover around the door at just the time that their masters were returning home—but still well before the sounds of the family car or their owner's footsteps could possibly be heard. Sometimes the dogs became alert when their master was more than a mile away and just beginning to start for home. Since these tests were often conducted on weekends or at irregular hours, this response was not just a matter of telling time (such as having their master return from work at a predictable time each evening).

According to folk traditions, the dogs with the highest degree of psychic ability are the "four-eyed dogs": light-colored dogs with a dark spot over each eye, or black dogs with light spots over each eye. Even today, on the Aegean island of Icaria, there are some people who always take four-eyed dogs with them to warn them if they come near a Nereid. Nereids are sea nymphs who are beautiful but dangerous. On land they lure men over cliffs to their deaths, while at sea they lure boats dangerously close to rocks.

*D*o dogs have a special sense that allows them to find their way back to their family? This is the basis of one of the most famous and loved of all dog stories, *Lassie Come Home* by Eric Knight. In it, Lassie is sold to the Duke of Rudling. She escapes from his harsh kennel keeper and begins a journey that will take many weeks and will go from Scotland to Yorkshire—a distance of four hundred miles. While Lassie is fictional, Knight had drawn his inspiration from a newspaper article.

There are many such true stories. In October of 1988, the Hutchinson family moved from Niagara Falls, New York, to Indianapolis, leaving their four-year-old beagle, Oscar, behind to live with a grandson who was fond of him. In May 1989, seven months later, Oscar arrived at the Hutchinson's new home in Indiana. He was thin and bedraggled, with sore, blood-stained paws, after traveling more than a hundred miles farther than the fictional Lassie. Most amazing was the fact that Oscar had never left his neighborhood in Niagara Falls in his entire life!

How did Oscar find his way? Perhaps Eric Knight had it right when he wrote about how Lassie managed to choose the correct direction home: "Do not ask any human being to explain how she should know this. Perhaps, thousands upon thousands of years ago, before man 'educated' his brain, he too had the same homing sense: but if he had it, it is gone now."

CHAPTER 3

What Do Dogs Feel?

*A*sk the average person how to tell whether a dog is happy, and they will advise you to look at its tail—if the dog is happy, the tail is wagging. Unfortunately, this is only partly true. Rapid tail wagging, where the side-to-side swings are not very large, is actually a sign of excitement rather than pleasure. It is when the tail wags broadly at a moderately fast rate that the dog is trying to say either "I'm pleased" or "I like you."

Some tail wags have totally different meanings. A slight wag with the tail held at its normal height, for example, usually appears when greeting someone. It can be interpreted as "Hello there," but can mean "I see you looking at me. You like me, don't you?"

A slow wag with the tail held lower than its usual height is a sign of insecurity. It often shows up when a dog is working on a problem—trying to understand what is going on. During dog training, I interpret this signal as "I'm trying to understand you. I want to know what you mean, but I can't quite figure it out." Once the dog finally solves the problem, the speed and size of the tail wags will usually increase until it becomes the broad wag that we interpret as happiness.

*T*ail wagging is similar to a human smile in that it is a social signal meant to communicate an emotional state to someone else. Most of us think that smiles are automatic and burst forth whenever we are feeling good—whether alone or in a crowd. However, psychologists have used hidden cameras to show that humans usually don't smile unless there is somebody around to see them. The one exception is the occasional smile we get when somebody special is present in our thoughts.

Using the same technique, psychologists have learned that dogs reserve their tail wags for living things. A dog will wag its tail for a person or another dog and may do so for a cat, horse, mouse, or even a moth. If the dog is alone, however, it simply doesn't wag its tail. Thus, when you give a dog a bowl of food, it will wag its tail to say, "Thank you. You've made me happy." If it walks into an empty room and then finds its bowl full of food, however, the tail wagging doesn't occur (other than, perhaps, a slight tremor that seems impossible to suppress). Furthermore, evolutionary biologists have noticed that many breeds of dogs, as well as jackals, wild dogs, dingos, and some wolves have a distinctive white or dark tip at the ends of their tails. These scientists believe that the markings are designed to render tail wagging more visible to the other living things that they are wagging at.

*A*lthough people may have difficulty recognizing a dog's emotions, they certainly have little trouble expressing their own emotions to dogs. One odd piece of research showed that 63 percent of dog owners admitted to kissing their dogs. Where? you ask. Some 45 percent kissed their dogs on the nose, 19 percent on the neck, 7 percent on the back, 2 percent on the legs and 5 percent on the stomach. An additional 29 percent listed the place that they kiss their dog as "other." The researchers didn't ask where "other" was, and I don't even want to speculate.

*W*hile 63 percent of people admit that they kiss their dogs, only 51 percent say that they allow their dog to return the affection by licking their faces. For some unknown reason, married men over the age of forty-five are the group least likely to allow this kind of loving to occur.

Many of us can find physical evidence of our affection for dogs in our wallets or purses. Market researcher Barry Sinrod found that 87 percent of all people carry some kind of pictures of them in their wallets. Of those, 75 percent carry snapshots of their kids and 55 percent have one of their spouse. Some 40 percent carry photos of their dogs—that is 20 times more frequent than pictures of their mother-in-law, which were carried by only 2 percent of all the people surveyed.

A dog's mind can grasp such basic feelings as joy, anger, fear and excitement. Yet there are other, more complex emotions belonging only to humans that are quite foreign to dogs. One such emotion is guilt. Dogs do not worry about morality, scruples, ethics, principles, standards or virtue. The pendulum of a dog's mind oscillates between possible and impossible, not right and wrong.

For instance, I had an old cairn terrier (by the name of Flint) who was a continuous source of exasperation to my wife, Joan. She would shoo him off a chair, only to see him immediately jump up on the sofa. She would push him off one side of the bed, only to have him jump back upon the other side. She would scold him for barking at the door, only to have him jump up and begin barking at the window. One day when some company was visiting, Flint wandered around the room, nosing at the visitors in the hope that one of them might scratch his ear or perhaps drop a bit of food. With some concern that he might be annoying her guests, Joan waved him away, saying "Flint, stop bothering these people. Go find something interesting to do."

Flint took Joan at her word. He darted out of the room, then reappeared a few minutes later carrying one of her undergarments, flagrantly snapping it from side to side with great joy—to the amusement of the company and the dismay of my wife. As with many dogs, Flint's motto was, "If two wrongs don't make a right, try three."

*B*ecause they know the world is filled with duplicity, dogs do not attempt to guide their lives by any ethical principles. They often feel that what is right today might well be wrong tomorrow, or what is correct behavior for some favored few is considered improper for the unfavored majority. If you move to press them for an example they will undoubtedly demonstrate that what is considered immoral or criminal behavior for dogs is often the logical extension of activities that are considered perfectly respectable for cats.

Sometimes, no matter how hard dogs try, they can't seem to understand human values and rules. Take the case of a woman who came to me to ask for help with a housebreaking problem. "My husband gets really angry if our dog Arthur has an accident. When he caught Arthur messing the floor in the kitchen he yelled at him. Then he grabbed the dog and threw him out of the open window into the back yard. This happened several more times during the week. Now when Arthur feels the need to relieve himself he goes into the kitchen, messes in the middle of the floor, and then jumps out of the window! What do we do next?"

*D*ogs know one aspect of human emotion very well—that they bring hope and comfort to humans just by being near them. A seaman who was with the British Royal Navy during World War II told me a story about a mixed-breed dog named Daisy who was the mascot of a Norwegian trawler. Daisy spent most of her time in the wheelhouse while the ship was fishing in the North Sea. One night, without any warning, a German U-boat torpedoed the ship and blew it to bits. By the light of the burning wreckage survivors managed to find each other, and they congregated in a little knot, struggling to keep afloat in the darkness. Through the black night, Daisy paddled from one sailor to another. She would stop at each crewman, appear to check on his condition, and lick his face.

The seaman told me: "It was as if she was reassuring each man, and telling them that they would make it if they only didn't give up. They had been in the water for several hours when my ship picked them up. We put them ashore back in England. All that they seemed to want to talk about was Daisy. They said that it was her presence that kept them going and kept their spirits up, even though they had little hope of being rescued." When the Royal Society for the Prevention of Cruelty to Animals heard of the story they commemorated Daisy's courage and compassion with a medal.

*D*ogs do know fear. It is a useful emotion; it keeps them from trying to leap wide chasms or hunt semi-trailers on the highway. The greatest fear dogs know, however, is the fear that you will not come back when you go out the door without them.

One of the oddest delusions we have is the notion that friendships should be lifelong. The truth of the matter is that humans are quite flexible about this issue. As people age and change, many wear out their friendships as they wear out their clothes, their political beliefs and their love for loud music. Only the friendship between a dog and a person seems to have the resilience to withstand all of these changes.

CHAPTER 4

What Is a Dog's Nature?

*D*ogs do not write, so there are no diaries to tell what an individual dog has learned. Dogs do not have museums and libraries to display and conserve any erudition, culture and discernment that they have acquired as a species. Dogs simply store all of their wisdom in their genes.

Even scientists are amazed at how much of a dog's behavior is genetically controlled. Dalmatians, for example, were originally bred to run under a horse-drawn carriage, and then to guard it when it was parked (you might call them the first car alarm). The "ideal coaching position" was when the dog ran under the front axle of the carriage, very close to the heels of the rear horses—the closer the better. Dogs who ran under the center of the carriage or under the rear axle were in "poor coaching position."

When Harvard University researchers looked at twenty-five years of kennel breeding records, they found that mating two dogs who both ran in good coaching position was much more likely to produce a dog that also ran in a good coaching position. Puppies produced by mating a dog with good coaching position and one with bad coaching position were less dependable. The worst case came from mating two dogs with bad coaching position dogs. (This was fairly rare since, as might be expected, the kennel had no interest in developing a line of Dalmatians that automatically assumed bad coaching positions.)

*B*ecause so much of a dog's behavior is determined by its genetic makeup, its breed becomes an important means of predicting its nature. Indeed, the central concept of a "purebred" dog involves controlling a dog's genetic makeup through selective breeding.

Knowing a dog's breed is a good way to predict its activity level, intelligence and personality. For example, spaniels tend to be the most loving of dogs, followed by retrievers. Working dogs like German shepherds, Doberman pinschers, and collies tend to be sober citizens who are willing to be friendly, but don't like overt "kissy-face" kinds of behavior. Terriers tend to be feisty and standoffish, and some breeds of hounds are only barely willing to acknowledge that humans exist.

A man once told me that his dog was half pit bull and half poodle. He claimed that it wasn't much good as a guard dog, but it was a vicious gossip.

*E*ach breed of dog has its own unique set of characteristics and personality traits that make it special. For instance:

An Airedale believes that it is of no use to anyone unless it provokes a furor.

Each year, a healthy Jack Russell terrier consumes one and a half times his weight in human patience.

Bulldogs display that typically English characteristic for which there is no English name.

All poodles act as if they have won first prize in the lottery of life.

All spaniels have a way of getting the answer "yes" without ever having posed any clear question.

The Chihuahua's greatest ambition is to live in a hot country and watch its master throw stones in the sea.

Golden retrievers are not dogs—they are a form of catharsis.

The beautiful and elegant Afghan hound knows two things: first, it is not very smart; second, it doesn't matter.

*T*he issue of a dog's personality also contributes to the popularity of the breed. It is interesting to note that the most popular dog breeds (in terms of the number of purebred dogs registered with kennel clubs) have remained fairly constant in the United States and Canada. Over the last few years, the top ten breeds of dogs have consistently included a substantial guard dog (the Rottweiler), a friendly, family dog (the Labrador retriever) and the elegant and adaptable poodle. In a typical year, the American Kennel Club will register more than thirty thousand litters of each of these breeds.

Some dogs go in or out of fashion depending upon their star status—for instance: Lassie moved collies out of pastures and into many living rooms and the beagle's popularity has probably been forever assured by Snoopy. Whether Dalmatians are in the top ten breeds or not seems to depend upon how recently Disney has released some version of the movie *101 Dalmatians*. At the time of this writing, the ten most popular breeds in the Western world are as follows: (1) Labrador retriever, (2) Rottweiler, (3) poodle, (4) German shepherd, (5) Dachshund, (6) golden retriever, (7) cocker spaniel, (8) beagle, (9) Pomeranian, (10) Yorkshire terrier.

Some dogs have become extremely rare because they were simply too good at their jobs. Take the Scottish deerhound, a breed used for hunting Scottish deer (which could stand over five feet at the shoulder). When Scottish deerhounds had hunted their prey to extinction, the breed lost its major function in life.

Other dogs have seen their popularity fade simply because their star status has waned. The distinctive and rugged Dandie Dinmont terrier owed its original popularity to Sir Walter Scott's book *Guy Mannering*, a best seller in 1814. This book is virtually unread today, and so we seldom see Dandie Dinmonts any more. In some cases, the diminished popularity of a breed is a fashion statement. For example, despite its working ability, intelligence and pleasant manners, to many people the Irish water spaniel looks like a mutant poodle with a rat's tail.

Of the more than half a million purebred litters registered by the American Kennel Club each year, some breeds will account for only two or three dozen litters each. In fact, some recognized breeds of dogs are now so rare that if they were wild animals, they would probably be on the International Endangered Species List. Such breeds include otterhounds, Irish water spaniels, Scottish deerhounds, Sealyham terriers, Ibizan hounds, Dandie Dinmont terriers, Pharaoh hounds, and Sussex spaniels.

*D*ogs seem to know more about their breeding than do most humans. Take the case of Steven and Barbara Kaufman of New York City. On a European holiday, they visited a small village near the Alps where a man offered to sell them a puppy from a litter of Tyrolean mountain dogs. The Kaufmans had never heard of this breed before. When the man showed them the litter, he explained that this was an extremely rare type of dog bred only in this region of the world. He explained that "these dogs grow to be quite large, and their big wide paws and phenomenal strength give them the ability to climb mountains and deal with snow and ice conditions extremely well." The Kaufmans fell in love with these cinnamon-colored tailless puppies, with their fat paws, blunt faces and round ears, and decided to make the purchase. The asking price was quite steep, but they felt this was to be expected for such a rare breed. As part of the sale, they received an ornate certificate with their puppy's kennel name and breed.

The Kaufmans named the dog Piton, after a piece of climbing equipment. Once back in New York, though, they found that Piton was growing at a phenomenal rate and eating quite voraciously. He was also becoming a bit aggressive, especially when they tried to cut his quickly growing toenails. At this point, the Kaufmans decided to take Piton to the veterinarian for a nail trimming. When they hauled him onto the examining table, Barbara proudly told the vet, "I'll bet you haven't run into many animals like this before." The vet nodded and said, "That's certainly true. This is the first time I have been asked to treat anybody's pet bear!"

Sometimes it can be unwise to try to modify a dog's nature. This can be seen in dog shows where beauty, physical soundness and conformation to breed standards are assessed. Shows were designed to identify dogs that are the best examples of their breed, so that the finest dogs can be bred to produce puppies with the most desirable characteristics. Since the ability to breed is important, dogs that enter in the shows must be intact (not spayed or neutered), and male dogs must have two normal testicles. A dog with only one testicle descended into the scrotum is called a *monorchid,* while one where neither has descended is called a *cryptorchid.* Either condition will result in disqualification. Fortunately for some dogs, such problems correct themselves over time, and the testicles do eventually descend so that the dog can be shown.

There is a story of a man who owned what he believed was a particularly handsome young Rottweiller. Unfortunately, it was a cryptorchid whose testicles had failed to descend. He wanted to enter this dog in a specialty show in Philadelphia in order to impress some friends. At great expense, he had a veterinarian give the animal testicular implants (for cosmetic reasons, he assured the vet). A couple of months later the dog was entered in the Philadelphia show. While in the ring, the judge was amazed to find that this Rottweiler had four testicles instead of two. Its owner had missed the fact that, just a few days before the show, the dog's natural testicles had descended to join the implants. The owner and his now too-masculine dog were summarily ejected from the show.

The genetic makeup of dogs provides some breeds with special abilities. I recently received a phone call from a Royal Canadian Mounted Police constable, who told me that he was associated with the new automated photo radar system that was being introduced to control speeding on the highway. The system is designed to measure the speed of vehicles passing the installation; if any of them exceed the posted speed limit by a specified amount, a photograph of the license plate is automatically taken. The car's owner is later sent a traffic ticket and a copy of the incriminating photo on which their excessive speed was recorded.

Puzzled, I asked why the police were contacting me about this issue. "Well," he said in a rather uncomfortable tone of voice, "we set up one of the first monitors near an elementary school with a posted speed limit of 20 kilometers per hour [around 15 mph]. The first two speeders caught by the system were something that looked like an Afghan hound and something that looked like a Doberman pinscher. We wanted to know whether this kind of speed was common enough in dogs to pose a problem for us."

Dogs certainly know how to run quickly, and many can reach speeds of 60 to 65 kph (35 to 40 mph) in short running bursts. The fastest greyhound ever clocked was Ballyregan Bob, who could run a kilometer in 40 seconds, which is 90 kph (over 56 mph). Dogs know, however, that as long as they are not wearing a license plate, they will never be fined for speeding.

CHAPTER 5

How Do Dogs Speak?

One of the most controversial questions about what a dog knows has to do with language and communication. Do dogs understand any of our speech? If so, how much? One researcher believes that dogs can quickly pick up the significance of various word sounds and certain signals. According to him, an average house dog, (only trained for basic obedience commands) can probably interpret the equivalent of 60 to 140 words.

I received a letter from a German dog trainer who claimed that he had taught a German shepherd to respond to almost 350 words. "These words do not have to be one or two-word commands," he wrote, "but can be part of a sentence. The dog just picks out the important part and does what he is required to do." Although I have not actually seen this dog perform, let us accept this report as some evidence that dogs can understand some of the complex aspects of human language.

The next question is whether dogs can speak. Dogs don't have the ability to control their tongues and vocal cords to form human word sounds very well. They have only a tail to wag, ears to flap and a tongue to lick with, so it is unfair to expect them to create poetry. Yet, in the absence of the spoken word, dogs do communicate. When my dog sits and listens to me tell him about complex problems and then gently beats his tail against the floor, I know that this really means, "You're getting closer to the answer. Keep at it and I'll let you know when you're there."

common belief held by many African, Australian, Native American and Haitian peoples is that dogs can understand every word we say. According to these folk beliefs, not only can dogs understand speech, but they actually have the ability to talk under certain circumstances—if they have a particular reason to do so. For instance, there is an Irish legend that gives us the good news that there is a way for people to understand dogs if they talk. The Speech of a dog becomes interpretable only if the listener is standing directly in front of the dog while wearing a four-leaf clover. The bad news is that dogs only feel the need to talk just before a disaster.

*A*ccording to some folk tales, dogs know how to speak but simply choose not to. In Africa, for example, the Nyanga people tell a story that many years ago a great hero named Nkhango struck a deal with the dog, Rukuba. If Rukuba stole some fire from the god Nyamurairi and gave it to Nkhango, all dogs would earn man's eternal friendship. The dog kept his part of the bargain and gave man fire. Later, Nkhango enlisted Rukuba's help in hunting. Together they successfully killed such dangerous prey as wild boars and lions. Soon, because of the dog's intelligence, Nkhango began to entrust him with more and more tasks.

Finally, Nkhango decided to use the dog as a messenger. This was too much for Rukuba. All that the dog really wanted was to lie by the fire in comfort, and since he had given humans fire, he felt that it was his right to do so. Rukuba concluded that men would always be sending him to this place or that on errands, because he was clever and could speak. Then the dog thought, "If I could not speak, then I could not be a messenger." From that day on, dogs chose never to speak again.

Unfortunately, this decision did not actually save them from serving as messengers. The army of ancient Rome used dogs to carry messages between military units. Routine messages were placed in a small container attached to the dog's collar, while secret messages were placed in a small metal tube that the dog was forced to swallow. Unfortunately for Rukuba's descendants, the process of retrieving the latter messages involved killing the dog and opening its stomach. Perhaps if Rukuba had known what lay many years ahead, he might have reconsidered his vow of silence.

The American Animal Hospital Association carried out a survey of people's attitudes toward their pets. One of their questions was, "When you are away from home, do you ever talk to your dog on the phone or through your answering machine?" One third of all the dog owners contacted admitted that they did. The survey, however, did not ask people to tell them what their dog said in response to their phone messages.

Another published survey tried to answer the question of whether people think their dogs are talking to them when they bark, whine or whimper. Based on more than one thousand questionnaires, researchers found that 78 percent of dog owners think that their dogs are actually speaking to them. And what are these dogs saying? The people questioned felt that their dogs were telling them quite everyday things, like "It's time to let me out," "I want a walk," "Let's play," "Come here," "My water bowl is empty" or "I love you." Not one respondent mentioned that the dog was providing comments on ancient Oriental philosophy, politics, religion or the state of the economy.

*M*ost people certainly act as if they believe that their dog has a comprehensive knowledge of human language. Whether dogs understand our speech or not, they are wonderful listeners. One friend of mine tragically lost her husband just a few months after she learned that she was pregnant. She later admitted to me that talking to Gus, her golden retriever, was one of the things that helped her through her crisis. "I could sit and talk to him and he would stay close and just listen. I told him what my plans were, what I thought I would do next, and how I was feeling. He would listen and then lean against me as if he wanted to reassure me. I think I interpreted the fact that he was listening, and not getting upset or walking out of the room, as meaning that what I was doing was all right and what I was feeling was normal."

In our culture we don't find it all that strange when people talk conversationally to their dogs. In *The Wizard of Oz*, nearly half of Judy Garland's lines as Dorothy are addressed to Terry, the cairn terrier who played the role of Toto.

Scientists may accept the fact that dogs are good listeners, but they claim there is no proof to substantiate the stories suggesting dogs can talk. According to these researchers, if your dog tells you that he can talk, he's lying.

Some people believe that dogs really don't understand words, but do respond to the tone of your voice. Accordingly, if Fido responds to "Fido, roll over," he will also respond to "Hi-ho, goal blubber." This may reflect the dog's cleverness at being able to piece together the meaning of our often slurred and distorted speech. After all, when our mouth is full, "Lassie, come" is apt to come out as "Frassy, glum"—but Lassie arrives hopefully at the table nonetheless. That dogs respond to specific words, however, has been proven in psychological laboratories.

It was also proven by the actor Richard Burton, who was married to the actress Elizabeth Taylor. She was so fond of her many dogs that once, while shooting a film in England, Taylor insisted that they all live on a boat moored on the Thames. This way, her dogs never needed to step on the English shore and thus avoided the usual six-month period of quarantine.

Taylor felt that she could communicate better with her dogs than Burton could and somewhat to his annoyance, this seemed to be true. Such was the case until Burton bought her a Pekingese, named E'en So. The dog was blind in one eye and Burton claimed that he had "rescued" it. Although the dog seemed friendly enough, Taylor could never get it to respond as well to her as it did to Burton. It seemed to ignore her words and only pay attention to his. Burton later admitted that he had purchased the dog fully trained, but only to commands spoken in Welsh—a language that he spoke fluently.

ometimes dogs show unexpectedly good language comprehension. In the United States, the abolition of slavery came after a bloody civil war; if dogs kept their own history, they might recount that their period of slavery ended with the invention of mechanical and electrical motors. Many dogs were specifically bred as a compact source of cheap power. For example, meat was traditionally cooked over an open fire on horizontal spits that needed to be rotated to cook the meat evenly. The tedious job of turning the meat was given to a special breed of heavy, long-bodied and short-legged dogs, appropriately called turnspits. They were placed in an enclosed wheel, like the suspended wheels you sometimes see in hamster cages. The dog's walking generated the rotary motion needed to turn the metal spit attached to its center. A house might have several turnspits, and each might be required to work the wheel for a number of hours.

Turnspits were also used to generate the motion needed to churn butter, grind grains, and pump water. There is even a patent for a dog-powered sewing machine. When one or more of these dogs was not needed as a source of power, turnspits were often taken to church to serve as foot warmers.

One Sunday, the bishop of Gloucester was giving a service in Bath Abbey. He drew his text from the tenth chapter of the Book of Ezekiel, turning to the congregation at one point to shout, "It was then that Ezekiel saw the wheel." And at the mention of the word *wheel*—the turnspit's dreaded workplace—one witness reported that number of dogs "clapt their tails between their legs and ran out of the church."

CHAPTER 6

What Tales Do Dogs Tell?

*T*he Chinese zodiac contains only symbols of animals. One of these celestial animals is a dog, although we don't know its breed. Every twelfth year is the Year of the Dog. People born in 1910, 1922, 1934, 1958, 1970, 1982, 1994, for example, are all born under the sign of the Dog. According to Chinese astrologers, those born under this sign are said to be honest, loyal and champions of justice. They can also be stubborn, tend to worry too much, and are not fond of crowds or social gatherings. People born in the Year of the Dog tend to be successful as educators, writers, philosophers, doctors, scientists, judges, priests and (of course) critics.

Despite dogs' august astrological qualities, Mao Zedong banned them as pets in China during the Cultural Revolution of 1965. This resulted in the extermination of millions of dogs. Even today, the only way a person living in China can pet a Pekingese is by visiting a zoo.

*W*omen, dogs and spiritual beliefs all mix together in a strange custom—found in central India among certain of the Gond peoples. This leads to a ritual that actually accepts the marriage of a human to a dog. The Gond are aboriginal tribes that still speak a fairly obscure set of unwritten languages. Their lifestyle, while not truly nomadic, tends not to have permanent settlements. Villages are periodically moved to various sites on land communally owned by the clan. Gond beliefs place them outside of the Hindu caste system. They do not acknowledge the superiority of Brahmans and don't feel bound by many Hindu rules.

Especially in the highlands of Bastar, the Gond style of agriculture is quite traditional, involving slash-and-burn operations. Because they are continually clearing new land, they often encounter wild animals, and these encounters can be fatal to humans armed only with digging sticks or hoes. The Gond of Bastar believe that if a woman's husband has been killed by a wild animal, especially a tiger, it is necessary for her to marry a dog before she can take another husband. This is because the Gond believe that the dead husband's spirit now inhabits whatever killed him, and this spirit will then cause that same beast to kill any new man the woman marries. To solve this problem, the widow must first ceremonially marry a dog. The dead husband's spirit can then satisfy his jealousy by killing the dog, and thus he will not threaten the life of the next human husband. While this seems like a good outcome for the woman, I think that dogs would accept a simple divorce as a much better and healthier end to their marriage.

The relationships between dogs and women have occasionally been distorted by religious beliefs. Throughout Alaska and the Aleutian Islands (which extend from Alaska out into the Bering Sea) there were a number of tribes that believed that their god first came to earth in the form of a dog. It was believed that the first woman had ten children who were fathered by this dog. Five remained near where they were born and were the ancestors of all tribes of Indians, while the other five set to sea on a raft, and ultimately became ancestors to all other people in the world.

Prior to the arrival of Europeans, dogs were the only draft animals among almost all Indian tribes. They were required to drag household items from place to place on a travois—a kind of primitive vehicle consisting of two poles attached to a harness on the dog. The poles trailed on the ground behind the animals with a platform or basket strung between them. At certain times in the year, out of respect for the Creator's dog form, the Chippewa Indians of south-central Canada would not use dogs for their usual transport and hauling functions. During those periods of time the dogs were allowed to run free and the women of the tribe were required to pull the travois.

*D*uring World War I, Colonel H. E. Richardson founded the first British dog school designed to train dogs for specialized military tasks. When the call for canine recruits went out, the number of dogs "volunteered" by their owners was astounding; nearly seven thousand dogs were offered to the army in the first two weeks.

With so many recruits, Richardson needed some way to separate dogs that were best suited to be "war dogs" from those that were not likely to be useful. One of his selection criteria was based upon observation of the dog's tail. Colonel Richardson claimed that dogs who carried their tails curled jauntily over their backs rarely had any value for military purposes. "This method of carrying the tail seems to indicate a certain levity of character, quite a variance from the serious duties required."

*I*n World War II the Allies needed dogs for many purposes. In the United States alone, well over fifty thousand dogs were enlisted, and five War-Dog Reception and Training Centers were established by the U.S. Army Quartermaster Corps.

The most common use for dogs was in sentry work, but they found themselves employed in a wide variety of jobs. Some were used to lay telephone wire, to carry packs, or to haul ammunition and guns; others served as scouts and even artillery or gun spotters. Some continued their civilian chores, such as keeping the rat population down in army camps and in front-line foxholes and trenches.

Others were trained for delicate and dangerous tasks, including mine detection. Dogs became an especially important means of finding land mines after the Germans introduced nonmetalic plastic mines in North Africa, since these devices were completely invisible to traditional magnetic mine detectors. Perhaps the most exotic occupation was held by dogs who were trained as spies. They were taught to infiltrate enemy camps to steal documents. Despite advice like that of Colonel Richardson, almost all breeds of dog were drafted by the U.S. Army. In fact, the only breed explicitly refused by war-dog recruiters was the basset hound.

*D*ogs have played many roles during human warfare, some important and some minor. General George Washington, who became the first president of the United States, had a special fondness for dogs.

Washington was avidly interested in fox hunting, so it is not surprising that his major interest was in hounds. They became his hobby, and his diaries are filled with accounts of his dog breeding. Washington's feelings about these dogs can be detected in the names that he gave them, including Sweetlips, Venus, and Truelove. (These shared a kennel with dogs named Taster, Tippler and Drunkard, but we don't have time for a psychological analysis of another love indicated by these names.) After the American Revolutionary War, French General Marquis de Lafayette acknowledged Washington's passion by sending him a pack of five hounds as a gift.

Washington's affection for dogs is vividly illustrated in an incident that occurred during the war. American forces were trying to contain British general William Howe's troops, which had occupied New York City. During the Battle of Long Island (which went badly for the Americans), General Howe's little terrier became lost between the lines. The dog was identified from its collar and brought to General Washington. He kept the dog in his tent to feed him, and afterward he ordered a cease fire. Soldiers on both sides watched silently as one of Washington's aides formally returned the little dog to the British commander under a flag of truce.

It is probably the case that few dogs know there is a holiday set aside for them—the third of November, which is the feast day of Saint Hubert, the patron saint of dogs. Hubert was the son of the Belgian Duke of Guienne. As a young man, he was boisterous and self-indulgent, and he dearly loved to hunt. His redeeming grace was his love of dogs.

The story is that he and some friends irreverently took their hounds out to hunt on Good Friday in 683 A.D. During the hunt, the dogs suddenly stopped their pursuit and reverently lay down in front a great white stag. When the stag turned, Hubert saw the image of the Cross between its antlers and heard the voice of God telling him that it was time to begin to hunt for virtue. Shortly thereafter Hubert took holy orders, established an abbey, and eventually rose to be a bishop of the church. At the abbey he continued to breed dogs and created the Saint Hubert hound, from which our modern bloodhounds have descended.

In early November, some years ago, I was traveling through rural North Carolina. I stopped when I came upon a large crowd standing in front of a church. The crowd consisted of all kinds of people and dogs: children with pets, shepherds with sheepdogs, and hunters with hounds. The priest mounted the church steps, dressed in white robes, and proceeded to give the "Mass of the Dogs" in honor of Saint Hubert. At the end the oldest dog was called up and blessed, and then every dog in turn received a benedictory touch from the priest. I am certain that no dog present barked even once during the entire proceedings. Actually, according to my recollection, many dogs seemed to bow their heads respectfully during the prayer service.

For some reason, there has always been a link between dogs and Christmas. Perhaps it's because the Christian account of the birth of Jesus has him surrounded by shepherds. Since shepherds require dogs, it has become traditional to show dogs along with the people gathered around the manger in Nativity scenes. In Grenada, Spain, a tale is told about three dogs who followed the three shepherds into Bethlehem. When they found the infant Jesus, the dogs were given the opportunity to gaze upon him, and they were blessed by the holy Infant's smile. Because the dogs' names were Cubilon, Lubina and Melampo, many people in Grenada still give their dogs these names as sort of a good-luck charm.

Lyndon Baines Johnson, former president of the United States, loved both dogs and Christmas. He even went so far as to have Christmas cards made up that featured a picture of him with two of his dogs—his white collie, Blanco, and one of his beagles, Him. The card was signed with Johnson's signature and the pawprints of the two dogs. On his last Christmas in the White House, Johnson's mood was light, even though Richard Nixon (whom Johnson despised) would soon be replacing him as president. Yuki, the president's well-loved white terrier, was decked out as Santa Claus, with a red coat and a proper hat; sniffing around the tree, he suddenly stopped and lifted his leg. Johnson laughed as he removed a now-wet box from the pile of gifts and announced, "I suppose that Santa has just told us which present he wants to give to President Nixon!"

oan Dyck of Chicago tells another holiday tale about her Shetland sheepdog. "I suppose that she was meant to be a Christmas elf from the beginning. My husband gave her to me as a Christmas gift, so I named her Noel. A year later, our daughter Rebecca was born. When Becky was around three and a half years old, we moved away from the center city region, to a real house. We could now have Christmas with a tree in front of a real fireplace. Becky was worried about whether Santa Claus would fit down the chimney, but we explained to her that Santa was magic, and could shrink himself down to elf size. We also warned her that she had to stay in her room, since Santa wouldn't give gifts to children if he saw them out of bed when he came.

Christmas Eve came, and when Becky was asleep we set up the tree. Around midnight Becky burst into our bedroom and woke us, crying, 'I saw Santa! Is he going to take away my presents now?' While her father comforted her, I cautiously sneaked downstairs. There in the empty fireplace sat Noel, shaking a fancy red Christmas stocking in order to get some candies out of it. To Becky's sleepy little eyes, he was Santa. That was twelve years ago, and I have still found no need to tell her otherwise."

CHAPTER 7

What Do Dogs Do?

*D*ogs are not just kept as companions; many have jobs and specific functions. The dog's sense of loyalty and its natural instinct to defend its territory make it an ideal watchman and guard. Breeds like the Doberman pinscher, German shepherd or virtually any terrier do not have to be trained to be watchdogs. These dogs will automatically sound the alarm at any disturbance near their home. (Of course, there will be false alarms as well, such as when the wind causes tree branches to brush against the house at two in the morning.)

Experts say any list of the top watchdogs should include Rottweilers, German shepherds, Doberman pinschers, all terriers (from the large Airedale to the tiny Yorkshire terrier), schnauzers of all sizes, poodles, Shih-Tzus and surprisingly the tiny Chihuahua, who will loudly sound the alarm when any stranger approaches. Other breeds take a more relaxed approach; for instance, dogs like the Labrador retriever know that the best watchdogs can guard the household simply by choosing some appropriate place to sleep. With the right choice, in the darkness, a burglar is bound to inadvertently trip over them with a loud clatter, thus alerting the family.

One day a man showed up at my university office with a videotape that he wanted me to see. "I know that in one of your books you said that Chihuahuas were good watchdogs, and will bark to warn about anything unusual. On the other hand, you also said that they were no good as guard dogs, since there was no way that such a little dog could actually protect you if someone was out to hurt you. Well, the reason that I am here is that I want to show you that you were wrong. While I was in Mexico I visited a man who trains Chihuahuas as guard dogs." I watched with amazement as the video played. It showed a man wearing a padded suit, like that used to train attack dogs. He was acting the part of a thief and stealthily opening a garden gate. Suddenly a pack of about a dozen tiny dogs swarmed all over him, biting, slashing and barking.

"This is all very impressive, but wouldn't it be more efficient just to have one big Rottweiler or a Doberman pinscher?" I asked. "Not at all," the man said. "It only takes one gunshot or a good hit with a club to disable a single big guard dog. With a pack of ten or more Chihuahuas, the intruder can't stop them all. He wouldn't have enough bullets, and they would incapacitate him before he could club every one of them. You see, they are trained to just keep biting and slashing, like a school of piranha fish." I suppose that I had just learned a fact that dogs already know: the important thing is not the size of the dog in the fight, but the size of the fight in the dog.

*D*ogs certainly know how to guard their masters, but sometimes they misinterpret threats. In 1530, King Henry VIII sent the Earl of Wiltshire to visit the Pope. The earl had a petition requesting annulment of Henry's marriage to Catherine of Aragon; Henry wanted this annulment so that he could marry his newest heartthrob, Anne Boleyn.

The Earl of Wiltshire took his toy spaniel with him to the audience. When the pontiff extended his foot so that the kneeling earl could kiss his toe—as was the custom at the time—the spaniel interpreted this as an attempt to kick her master's face. The dog immediately leapt forward and protectively bit the holy digits.

Given the havoc that ensued, it is not surprising that the divorce was not granted. As a result, Henry VIII broke away from the Roman Catholic Church and formed the Church of England, which had a more liberal attitude toward granting him freedom from his wife.

*D*ogs do many things to help people. One of their most unusual functions involves assisting in psychotherapy.

This all started with Sigmund Freud, who had a series of dogs, most of them chow-chows. Freud felt that dogs had a special sense that allows them to judge a person's character accurately. For this reason his favorite chow-chow, Jo-Fi, attended all of his therapy sessions; Freud admitted that he often depended upon Jo-Fi for an assessment of the patient's mental state. He also felt that the presence of the dog seemed to have a calming influence on all patients, particularly children.

More recent studies have shown that Freud was correct. Physiological measures show that petting a calm and friendly dog actually reduces stress (as shown by reduced muscle tension, more regular breathing and a slower heart rate). There is even some evidence that people who own dogs are likely to live longer and require less medical attention.

Freud's dog Jo-Fi would alert him to any stress or tension in a patient by where he lay down during the session. He lay relatively close to calm patients, but would stay across the room if the patient was tense. Jo-Fi also helped the great psychoanalyst determine when a therapy session was finished by unfailingly getting up and moving toward the office door when the hour was up. Freud, however, denied the rumor that Jo-Fi actually did the therapeutic psychoanalysis and wrote up the case reports.

n most places in the Western world, laws only acknowledge the value of dogs as if they were just another form of property. One newspaper article, for example, reported the case of one Else Brown, a 67 year-old widow, whose dog, Tilly, was killed by a neighbor in a drunken act of aggression. The court ruled that this was not an assault, but just a crime against property, which would be treated like simple vandalism—the equivalent of breaking a window. Thus Tilly's murderer was simply given a fine equal to the cost of the dog (just a pitiful few dollars, since she had been adopted from an animal shelter). The years of love and caring, the loss of companionship had no dollar value in the eyes of the law.

Dogs know that you can buy them if you have enough money. It will take more than money, however, to buy the wag of their tails.

*E*ven as property, though, dogs have influenced many aspects of history. Just about everyone knows the story of Jamestown, the first permanent British settlement in Virginia. We tend to think of it as the story of the Indian maiden Pocahontas, but the settlement's survival is really also is a story about dogs, not as companions but as trade goods.

Jamestown was founded in 1607 but was viciously attacked by the Algonquin Indians, and nearly half the colonists were dead in the first six months. The colony was saved by several events. The first was the famous intervention of Pocahontas to save Captain John Smith from execution by her father, Chief Powhatan. The second was the arrival of a supply ship containing 100 fresh settlers, much-needed food, tools and of—equal importance—dogs. The British wanted gold, which had been discovered in the nearby Carolinas and Georgia, as well as fur, tobacco and Indian corn. Good hunting dogs were considered much more precious than gold by the Indians, since they had not yet mastered the technique of specialized dog breeding for hunting skills. The British hunting dogs became such a major consideration that they were specifically mentioned in the 1657 treaty that ended the conflict between Powhatan's Algonquins and the colonists. The central role of dogs in forging the peace is still celebrated by a dog parade and canine sports events in the annual October Dog Mart Day in Fredericksburg Virginia, although it seems to have been overlooked in recent Hollywood films about Pocahontas.

$\mathcal{D}$ogs know that they are often prized for some completely utilitarian reasons. For example, in North America, prior to the arrival of the Europeans, there were no domestic sheep. The Northwestern coastal Indians therefore developed a remarkably shaggy breed of dog simply for its fur, which was very soft and warm. When mixed with fur shed by wild goats, or with eiderdown or pounded cedar bark, it could be used to make excellent blankets and clothing. The British explorer Captain George Vancouver reported that in 1798, when he entered Puget Sound (in what is now the state of Washington), he was greeted by a pack of these dogs "all shorn as close to the skin as sheep are in England. So compact were their fleeces that large portions could be lifted up by a corner without causing any separation." Such dogs were often kept on small islands or in locked pens in order to prevent them from breeding with other dogs, whose fur was of lesser quality. Unfortunately, these "wool dogs" were put out of business by the Hudson's Bay Company when it introduced the Indians to mass-produced sheep's wool blankets.

Edith Wharton, the Pulitzer Prize–winning novelist who created classics like *Ethan Frome*, was once asked to make a list of the passions that ruled her life. First on this list was "justice and order," and second was "dogs." Dogs, of course, are sometimes a great aid in maintaining justice and order, working as patrol dogs and detecting drugs. Sometimes, however, they end up on the wrong side of the law.

A visiting scholar told me a story about his father in Hamburg, Germany, where well-trained guard and companion dogs can sell for very high prices. "My father was fond of German shepherds and had heard that there was a dog trainer and breeder named Hans Roehm who had splendid dogs. When he went to see Roehm, he was quite impressed, and bought a dog named Max from him. Max was very expensive, but he was very handsome and completely trained. Max had been with my father for only a week when he disappeared. Apparently he had run away. Advertisements in the paper had no success in finding the dog. Then, about a month later, my father saw a dog that looked exactly like Max. He stopped the owner and found out that this dog had also been purchased from Hans Roehm. When my father called Roehm, he was told that that dog was a litter mate of Max's, which was why his markings were so similar. Another month passed and my father again met the man who owned Max's brother. He did not have the dog with him, since it turns out that the dog had run away! My father was suspicious and contacted the police. An investigation found that Roehm was a very fine trainer indeed—he had trained his dogs to escape back to him as soon as they had a chance. Max had actually been sold nine times to nine different people!"

ometimes it's the dog himself who ends up in court. In 1976, in Grand Prairie, Texas, a six-year-old schnauzer named Max was put on trial. He was charged with breaking and entering and also with the rape of two pedigreed Pekingese females, named Dollie and Sen-Lee. Charges were brought by the owner of Dollie and Sen-Lee, George Milton; he was suing for damage to his house and for veterinarian fees to cover the abortions that were required after the assault. The judge, Cameron Grey, decided that Max was not guilty. As the basis of this ruling he cited a lineup that the police had held to identify the molester. At that time, Mr. Milton had confidently singled out a poodle as the assailant of his tiny dogs.

Sometimes both the dog and its owner end up in court. In 1996, in Waterbury, Connecticut, a local political activist named Barbary Monsky sued judge Howard Moraghan and his golden retriever, Kodak, for sexual harassment. Moraghan often brought his dog to Danbury Superior Court. According to Monsky, the dog had "nuzzled, snooped and sniffed" beneath her skirt at least three times, while the judge had done nothing about it. U.S. District Judge Gerard Goettel dismissed the case and in a later interview explained that "impoliteness on the part of a dog does not constitute sexual harassment on the part of the owner." The aggrieved woman responded by calling the decision "as insulting as having a dog sniff under a skirt."

CHAPTER 8

How Do Dogs Learn?

*D*ogs do learn. Perhaps the old folk proverb "Experience is the best teacher, and fools will have no other" explains why some people think dogs are lamentably crude or ignorant—after all, experience is the only teacher many dogs ever have.

As dogs grow older, though, their behavior does show that they have learned from their experiences. They become shrewder, more perceptive, and perhaps even a bit cunning. They develop the capacity to evaluate certain situations much more accurately. Thus for dogs, it is clear that judgment comes from experience, even if experience comes mostly from bad judgments. On the other hand dogs know that a life spent making mistakes is a lot more honorable than a life spent doing nothing at all.

recently received a card that said, "We certainly live a strange world, where kids run wild in the streets and dogs go to obedience classes." Obedience classes are quite common, and they are probably the closest thing to formal education that most dogs will ever encounter.

A recent survey examining how many dogs have gone to "school" found that only 24 percent of all dogs were ever given any formal obedience training. How well did this schooling work? Well, one out of every three dog owners said that either their pet flunked out of the class or they gave up before the class was over.

$\mathcal{D}$ogs who do well in obedience training have many opportunities to display their education. Most major kennel clubs have obedience competitions where a dog demonstrates its proficiency and knowledge.

In North America, dogs can earn three different obedience degrees. The Companion Dog (CD) degree requires the dog to perform some basic exercises that every civilized dog should be capable of, such as responding to "Sit," "Down" and "Stay" commands, coming when called, and walking beside his master in a controlled manner. The Companion Dog Excellent (CDX) degree requires the dog to obey these commands off leash, as well as performing tasks like jumping and retrieving on command. The highest degree, Utility Dog (UD), requires sophisticated behaviors like responding to hand signals instead of spoken commands, plus finding and retrieving items by scent alone.

One dog obedience judge admitted to me that sometimes, at a practical level, it is difficult to know whether a dog that won't sit, come, or fetch on command is too stupid to learn or too smart to bother.

When dogs know something, they usually do not consider alternative interpretations. For example, during World War II, the Germans trained their military dogs to respond to certain hand signals. One of these was the traditional command for "Sit"—an extended arm with the palm outward.

There is a report that Hitler once reviewed a military parade that included trained army dogs. As the dog handlers approached, the Führer gave the Nazi salute. The obedient dogs, seeing what they believed to be a familiar signal, instantly responded by sitting down. Of course, the troops immediately behind—who were moving with their eyes rigidly facing forward in the German marching style—promptly stumbled over them, resulting in a chaotic pile of dogs and people. The embarrassed dog handlers were forced to retrain the dogs to a new signal.

$\mathcal{D}$ogs know how to adapt to their environment. For example, they are smart enough to adjust their behavior to fit into a multicultural world without discriminating against other races, sexes, or even species.

Marvin Goldman of Brooklyn, New York, learned this after he brought home a young puppy named Willy. In his home, Goldman also had a female cat who had just given birth to a litter of kittens. The cat "adopted" Willy, treating him like one of her kittens—even to the point of washing him with her tongue. Willy responded by quickly learning cat culture, including the familiar cat habit of washing his paws with his tongue and then using them to clean his face and ears.

I am often bothered by my own limited knowledge. I feel uncomfortable around well-traveled people who know other tongues because I don't speak French, Russian, or Italian well enough even to pronounce common words from those languages. I'm just as ill at ease around more technologically oriented scientists. I can't tell the difference between a *quark* and a *quirk*, and all that I know about *black holes* is that things disappear inside of them (something like the way single socks disappear in the laundry, I guess). And I'm also self-conscious around my more artistic acquaintances. I know little of the history of the British novel, I have memorized no Shakespearean sonnets, I cannot name any Flemish Renaissance portrait artists, nor do I remember who came first, Leonardo da Vinci or Michelangelo.

My dogs, however, are quite comfortable around everybody. It may well be the case that the saving grace of dogs is that they don't know how much they don't know.

*W*hether dogs know it or not, they often rely more upon instinct than upon knowledge or education. During World War II, the Nazis stationed along the Maginot Line used dogs as messengers. The French soldiers tried to shoot these dogs, but they were difficult to hit because they moved so quickly and silently.

One French dog handler then tried an experiment, releasing a small female French messenger dog who had just gone into heat. As she had been taught, the French dog returned to her post later that evening. Trailing behind her were nearly a dozen normally obedient German Army dogs who had discovered something much more powerful than their military training.

It is difficult to know what overall goals or plans guide any particular dog's behavior. One woman told me that her dog Bullet, a retriever of sorts, engaged in very systematic behaviors that seemed to make no sense to her. Because she was tired of tripping over them, she had gathered together all of Bullet's dog toys and put them in a box in one corner of her kitchen. During the afternoon Bullet took out various toys to play with; at the end of the day, however, the woman found all of the toys neatly piled in a corner of the living room. Feeling that this was Bullet's way of suggesting where he wanted his toy box to be located, she moved the container to that corner. The next evening she found the toys stacked in yet a different corner. Thinking that the problem might be the box itself, she left the pile of toys where the dog had put them. The next night the toys had been moved to yet another corner. "I stopped worrying about the whereabouts of his toys," she said. "Each night he moves them somewhere else, but at least now they are always neatly stacked."

What she had missed was the fact that dogs believe that activity and movement is more important than plans or goals. Action is always preferable to inaction, even if the acts are without a specific guiding principle. You might say that dogs don't quite know where they are going, but they do know that they are on their way.

CHAPTER 9

Where Do Dogs Go?

*E*ventually all dogs, like all humans, reach the end of their journey. A letter from a friend read: "You know that she was just a four-footed ball of fluff with a high-pitched bark at one end and bad manners at the other. I suppose it is best that she didn't know how hard it would be on me when she went away, since she used to get very upset when I was unhappy. She was, after all, only an animal, so the depth of my own feelings surprised me. It was as if, with her going, she was carrying away with her so many years of my life. I suppose that what finally pulled me out of my depression was religion. I spoke to a priest about what I was feeling, and he said to me: 'Don't grieve so. You must always remember that as far as the Bible is concerned, God threw only the humans out of Paradise.'"

*A*re there dogs in Heaven? For those who love dogs, it would be the worst form of a lie to call any place where dogs were banned "Paradise." Certainly no loving God would separate people from their canine friends for eternity.

Robert Louis Stevenson, author of novels such as *Treasure Island,* declared, "You think dogs will not be in heaven? I tell you, they will be there before any of us." George Eliot, the English writer of *Middlemarch* and *Adam Bede,* asked: "Shall we, because we walk on our hind feet, assume to ourselves only the privilege of imperishability? Shall we, who are even as they, though we wag our tongues and not our tails, demand a special Providence and a selfish salvation?"

Then there was Saint Patrick, the patron saint of Ireland. Tradition says that he promised Oissain, the son of the great hero Finn MacCumhail, that for helping him Christianize the land he could have his hounds in Heaven.

Martin Luther, founder of the Protestant church, was once asked by a child whether her dog would be allowed in Heaven. He gently patted the dog's head and said, "Be comforted, little dog, thou too in the Resurrection shalt have a tail of gold."

I had a dream shortly after my old cairn terrier, Flint, died. In it Flint was lying beside the gates of Heaven, and an angel came out to ask him why he didn't come in. In the telepathic speech common to celestial beings, my dog answered, "Can't I just stay out here awhile? I'll be good and I won't even bark. You see, I'm waiting for someone that I miss very much. If I went in alone, it wouldn't be Heaven for me." I woke from that dream to find tears on my face.

In many places around the world, there is a belief that a dog's howl is a warning of a coming death. Some say that this dire signal only occurs at midnight. Others say that this death howl is quite unique, with the dog holding his head down instead of pointed toward the sky as in the usual howl. Many believe that a howling dog can actually drive the Angel of Death away—and so the howling dog is trying to prevent the death that it sees coming.

In many religions dogs are *psychopomps*. This means that when you die, it is a dog's job to escort you to the next world, protecting you and showing you the way. Yima, the Zoroastrian god, is said to have set two four-eyed dogs to guard Chinvat Bridge, which is known as the "Bridge of Decision" between this world and Heaven. These dogs are placed there because they, like all dogs, are good judges of character. It is said that will not let anyone pass on to Paradise who has deliberately harmed a dog in this world.

*D*ogs don't know about beginnings, and they never speculate on matters that occurred before their time. Dogs also don't know—or at least don't accept—the concept of death. Everyone probably knows the story of Greyfriars Bobby, the little Skye terrier in Edinburgh, Scotland, who would not admit the death of his master. After the funeral he would not leave the grave site, and for the next nine years he faithfully returned every day to lie by his master's resting place.

Bobby is not alone. Dr. Eisaburo Ueno, a professor at Tokyo University, owned Hachiko, an Akita who accompanied his master to the train station each day to see him off; the dog would return to the station each afternoon to greet his master. One afternoon Professor Ueno did not return— he had died in Tokyo. Hachiko waited at the station until midnight. The next day, and every day for nearly ten years thereafter, Hachiko came to the station and waited for his master. After the train came and the passengers dispersed, Hachiko would search the station carefully before slowly walking home alone.

With no concept of beginnings or endings, dogs probably don't know that for people, having a dog as a life companion provides a brief streak of light between two eternities of darkness.

$\mathcal{D}$ogs seem to be tuned to sense the elusive essence of what we call life. Take the case of Mickey, a Labrador retriever owned by William Harrison, and Percy, a Chihuahua that had been given to his daughter, Christine. Despite their size difference, the two dogs were good friends and playmates until one evening in 1983, when Percy ran out into the street and was hit by a car. While Christine stood by weeping, her father placed the dead dog in a crumpled sack and buried him in a shallow grave in the garden. The depression that had fallen on the family seemed to affect not only the humans but also Mickey, who sat despondently staring at the grave while everyone else went to bed. A couple of hours later, William was awakened by frantic whining and scuffling outside the house. When he investigated the noise he saw, to his horror, that the sack he had buried Percy in was now laying empty beside the opened grave. Next to it he saw Mickey, in a state of great agitation, standing over Percy's body—frantically licking his friend's face, nuzzling and poking at the limp form in what looked like a canine attempt to give the "kiss of life."

Tears filled the man's eyes as he watched this futile expression of hope and love. He sadly walked over to move Mickey away from the small dog's body when he saw what looked like a spasm or twitch. Then Percy weakly lifted his head and whimpered. Some deep sense in Mickey had sensed that there was a faint spark of life in the little dog, and his instinct to oppose death had told him what to do. For this act, the animal charity Pro-dog named Mickey its Pet of the Year.

*M*arsha Hamilton's golden retriever, Buzzby, had been a vital part of her life for eleven years. Marsha often said that she couldn't have made it without the dog. When a miscarriage ended her dreams of being a mother, Buzzby had stayed at home and comforted her. When her marriage broke up, Buzzby had been her therapist and confidant. Buzzby's emotional support got Marsha through the hard times when she went back to university to study commercial art, and later during the depressing search for permanent employment. Then, just a few months after she finally got the job that she had always dreamed about, Buzzby died.

Marsha had barely begun to cope with this loss when a freak accident put her in the hospital; a multi-vehicle highway accident had caused a truck carrying caustic chemicals to spill over her. She lay in the hospital with her face completely bandaged, an air vent down her mouth. No one could tell her whether her eyes were permanently damaged, or whether she would be able to talk normally again. Marsha was afraid.

On the second night, she felt a great weight settle beside her in bed. Her unbandaged left hand reached out and felt familiar long fur. It was a golden retriever, so much like Buzzby that she almost cried. He came for three nights, and she felt comforted and secure. On the next day doctors removed the bandages, and Marsha found that she could see. As soon as she could speak again, she asked whether she could see the dog that they had brought to her for visits. When she was told that there had been no dog, Marsha felt tears in her eyes. She knew in her heart that Buzzby had come back to help her one last time, when she needed him most.

CHAPTER 10

Do Dogs Know People?

*D*ogs do understand people—in many respects they know humans better than other humans do. For example, dogs know that if they forgive a person enough, they belong to that person (and that person belongs to them). This happens without any thought or regard as to whether either party likes it. It is a cosmic law called "squatter's rights of the heart."

*D*ogs must be forgiving to live with such a fickle species as humans. Take the case of the pit bull terrier. Before World War I, this breed was America's symbol of independent strength and security, and a picture of a pit bull appeared on posters declaring "Neutrality Without Fear." RCA's popular corporate logo featured Nipper, a pit bull listening to a phonograph recording.

Pit bulls were funny dogs, and they were supposed to have a sense of humor. Everybody laughed at Petey, the pit bull co-star of the "Li'l Rascals" movies. Nice people owned pit bulls, including Fred Astaire, Helen Keller, John Steinbeck and James Thurber. Of course there were occasional incidents, such as when President Theodore Roosevelt's pit bull, Pete, tore the trousers off of the French ambassador during a visit to the White House. Everybody knew that the incident did no permanent damage, though, and took it in good spirits.

All that has now changed. Today, amid lurid press accounts of dog attacks, pit bulls are in danger of being legislated out of existence. Laws often place restrictions on "pit bull or pit bull-like dogs," a phrase interpreted to mean any dog with a large head. One man told me that animal control officers came to his home citing reports that he walked his pit bulls around the neighborhood without the muzzle required by municipal legislation. He protested, showing them his two dogs: a boxer and a wrinkly Chinese Shar-Pei. Until they received a letter from his veterinarian these officials could not be convinced that these dogs did not fall into the pit bull category.

*D*ogs forgive the fact that human love is fleeting. Back in 1931, a 150-pound Saint Bernard named Prince Pluto lived in Newport Beach, California. Pluto would often go to the pier with his master, Richard Gunther, and then wander along the beach and socialize with the bathers who were there to enjoy the sun and waves.

On this particular day, six-year-old George Mades was playing at the ocean's edge. Straying from his parents' sight, he suddenly was caught by a series of large waves and dragged out into the deep water. The floundering child caught Pluto's eye, and in a moment the big, strong-swimming dog dashed into the water. Young George, despite his frantic flailing, was being drawn further from shore. When Pluto reached him, the child desperately grabbed at the dog, but missed. Pluto latched onto the boy's swimming trunks, however, and started dragging him to shore. The child eventually managed to climb onto Pluto's back as the great dog struggled back to dry land. When George's parents reached the scene, the terrified little boy's fingers had to be peeled forcibly from the dog's fur.

This, however, was not the first time that Pluto had saved a child from drowning—it was the *fifth* time. For his heroism in the saving of five lives, Prince Pluto was named "official lifeguard of Newport Beach" by the city council. He was given a department badge and a safety light attached to a harness (for protection from traffic, should he choose to make his rounds at night). He was also given the Latham Foundation's Gold Medal Award for animal heroism.

Today, however, should you visit the site of Pluto's heroic activities, you will be greeted by a large sign: "No Dogs Permitted On This Beach." Times change.

Still, of all of the animals, dogs are very special to us. One proof of this is that we only name special animals; few farmers will name their cows, chickens or sheep. To name an animal is to grant it unique identity, and to accept it as a friend or companion. The top ten dog names in the United States and United Kingdom are as follows:

	Males		Females
1	Max	1	Princess
2	Rocky	2	Lady
3	Lucky	3	Sandy
4	Duke	4	Sheba
5	King	5	Ginger
6	Rusty	6	Brandy
7	Prince	7	Samantha
8	Buddy	8	Daisy
9	Buster	9	Missy
10	Blackie	10	Misty

Surprisingly, the name Snoopy (the dog made famous by Charles Schultz's comic strip "Peanuts") does not appear in the top of the dog list; however, it was found in the top ten names for *cats*.

Some people name dogs for unique reasons. I was told of one woman who named her dog Banjo. It seems that her husband wanted a banjo to play folk music and had been hinting that it would make a great birthday present. She was worried, however, because she knew that he had absolutely no musical talent. So she bought him the dog and gave it to him, saying, "Now you have your own Banjo!"

A dog's name becomes a signal: he knows that the next sounds coming out of it's master's mouth are supposed to have some impact on his life. For instance, all of my dogs have two names. The first is their unique name (like Wiz, Flint or Odin), and the second is "Puppy." Thus when I yell "Puppies come," I expect all of my dogs within earshot to appear at a run.

Some other dogs have a more difficult time with their names. Consider the case of the Skye terrier owned by Robert Louis Stevenson, the author of such classics as *Treasure Island* and *The Strange Case of Dr. Jekyll and Mr. Hyde*. His poor little dog was initially named "Woggs," which was then changed to "Walter," and then changed again to "Watty," then changed once more to "Woggy" and finally changed to "Bogue."

Most dogs do not have such problems in identifying themselves. The vast majority of dogs in the world know their names quite well, based on its frequency of use and the variety of situations in which it occurs. Of course most dogs, if you asked what their name is, would tell you that they are called "No!"

*D*ogs know that they become a true member of their human family. Although dogs don't require any evidence for this, human researchers like to explore just how much of a family member dogs have become. One bit of proof comes from the fact that 38 percent of all dog owners admit that they have occasionally slipped and called their spouse by their dog's name. It is interesting to note that 25 percent of this same group have made a mistake in the opposite direction, calling their dog by their spouse's name. Women are most likely to make these particular errors, which may indicate that women see less of difference between their dog and their spouse than do men.

For better or worse, children seem to be much more distinguishable than their parents. Only 11 percent of pet owners admitted to ever having called their children by their dog's name.

*D*ogs know that they are often viewed by their owners as if they were children. Great care is taken with their care, including (as with kids) making sure that they are dressed appropriately for the weather and for social events. Surveys show that 86 percent of dog owners admit to sometimes adorning their dogs with scarves or ribbons. Sixty-two percent of dog owners admit that their dog owns a sweater, winter coat or raincoat (some own all three). As for dress-up times, 23 percent of owners say that they own a fancy leash or collar with jewels, sparkles or fancy embroidery, while 6 percent of dog owners say that they have occasionally put other sorts of jewelry on their dogs.

I have difficulty conceptualizing what this "other sorts of jewelry" might be. I certainly would refuse to put a gold earring on my spaniel, regardless of the fashion statement that it might make.

nother way that dogs are treated as children is seen when marriages break up. In 38 percent of divorce proceedings involving dog owners, neither party wanted to give up their four-legged "child." Just as in the case of human children, judges seem predisposed to grant custody to the woman, with 81 percent of the rulings going in favor of the former wife. Furthermore, when women won custody of the dog, their former spouses were granted visiting rights in a meager 11 percent of the cases. In those rare cases where the former husband was granted custody of the dog, however, his ex-wife was granted visitation rights in 83 percent of the proceedings.

While I'm on the subject of being separated from one's dog: according to Harper's Index, it is estimated that more than one million Americans have named their dogs as beneficiaries in their wills.

*P*eople know the depth of the bond between dogs and humans. It is felt in the heart each time our dog comes to us when we call it, or lies next to us, simply because it wants to share our company.

Many cultures have stories of how humans and dogs came to be together. My favorite is found in the tales of several tribes of American Plains Indians. It tells of a time long ago when God, the Great Spirit, had just finished creating the world and all of its inhabitants. Then the Great Spirit decided that it was time to separate the world of humans from the world of animals. He sent out a call to gather all the living creatures in the world together on a wide plain. When they had assembled, he drew a line in the ground; on one side of this line were humans, on the other were all of the other animals. Now, while everyone watched, the line began to deepen and widen. It became a great crack in the earth. Then this crack began to open, and a bottomless chasm began to form. The abyss continued to widen—and then, at the last moment, just before the gap became unbridgeable, the dog leapt over to stand by man.

The Nobel Prize-winning author Maurice Maeterlinck expressed these same feelings when he said, "We are alone, absolutely alone on this chance planet; and amid all the forms of life that surround us, not one, excepting the dog, has made an alliance with us."

$\mathcal{D}$ogs can only know what they can sense, and this is ultimately their saving grace. Some psychologists say that the origin of modern neurosis in people may well lie with the discoveries of Copernicus. They say that neurosis came about because science made humans feel small. It did this by showing people that the earth is not the center of the universe— instead, it is only a tiny speck floating in an immense void. It further attacked people's self-image by proposing the theory of evolution, which suggests that humans are somehow, not only related to apes but, in the distant past, to insects and even sea slime. Dogs are unaffected by these revelations simply because they don't care. Dogs have opted never to inquire why, how or whether. A dog's philosophy is simply to enjoy his food while it is on his plate.

Dogs may not know, or care, about the full extent of their own limitations. After years of carefully observing human beings, however, they certainly seem to know ours. One day my dog came over to me while I was working. He looked at me and seemed to say, "It is all very well to be able to write books, but can you waggle your ears?"

So can we total things up and determine what dogs really know? Probably not in a manner that a scientist or even a philosopher would accept. We may never fully understand how dogs see the world. We may never determine what dogs know about humans, or why dogs find our species to be so special. We may never understand what drives dogs to spend much of their lives doing things that they put humans in asylums for. We may also live our lives never comprehending why, impelled by a state of mind that is not to last, dogs often make irrevocable decisions.

Science may never fully comprehend the full extent of what dogs know about language, problem solving, the past, the future, God, time or philosophy. In the end, we must content ourselves with the fact that dogs know enough to be dogs—which is all that is really required of them.